A Note From Rick Renner

I am on a personal quest to see a "revival of the Bible" so people can establish their lives on a firm foundation that will stand strong and endure the test when the end-time storm winds begin to intensify.

In order to experience a revival of the Bible in your personal life, it is important to take time each day to read, receive, and apply its truths to your life. James tells us that if we will continue in the perfect law of liberty — refusing to be forgetful hearers but determined to be doers — we will be blessed in our ways. As you watch or listen to the programs in this series and work through this corresponding study guide, I trust that you will search the Scriptures and allow the Holy Spirit to help you hear something new from God's Word that applies specifically to your life. I encourage you to be a doer of the Word that He reveals to you. Whatever the cost, I assure you — it will be worth it.

> Thy words were found, and I did eat them;
> and thy word was unto me the joy and rejoicing of mine heart:
> for I am called by thy name, O Lord God of hosts.
> — Jeremiah 15:16

Your brother and friend in Jesus Christ,

Rick Renner

Miracles and the Supernatural Throughout Church History

Copyright © 2020 by Rick Renner
8316 E. 73rd St.
Tulsa, Oklahoma 74133

Published by Rick Renner Ministries
www.renner.org

ISBN 13: 978-1-68031-762-6

eBook ISBN 13: 978-1-68031-763-3

Rick Renner's guest during this series is Tony Cooke, founder of Tony Cooke Ministries in Tulsa, Oklahoma. Tony is a Bible teacher and author who travels and ministers with his wife, Lisa, strengthening churches and leaders. For more information, go to **tonycooke.org**.

How To Use This Study Guide

This five-lesson study guide corresponds to *"Miracles and the Supernatural Throughout Church History" With Rick Renner and Guest Tony Cooke* (Renner TV). Each lesson in this study guide covers a topic that is addressed during the program series, with questions and references supplied to draw you deeper into your own private study of the Scriptures on this subject.

To derive the most benefit from this study guide, consider the following:

First, watch or listen to the program prior to working through the corresponding lesson in this guide. (Programs can also be viewed at **renner.org** by clicking on the Media/Archive links.)

Second, take the time to look up the scriptures included in each lesson. Prayerfully consider their application to your own life.

Third, use a journal or notebook to make note of your answers to each lesson's Study Questions and Practical Application challenges.

Fourth, invest specific time in prayer and in the Word of God to consult with the Holy Spirit. Write down the scriptures or insights He reveals to you.

Finally, take action! Whatever the Lord tells you to do according to His Word, do it.

For added insights on this subject, it is recommended that you obtain Tony Cooke's book *Miracles and the Supernatural Throughout Church History*. You may also select from Rick's other available resources by placing your order at **renner.org** or by calling 1-800-742-5593.

TOPIC

Are Miracles Still for Today?

SCRIPTURES

1. **1 Corinthians 13:8-10** — ...But whether there be prophecies, they shall fail; whether there be tongues, they shall cease; whether there be knowledge, it shall vanish away. For we know in part, and we prophesy in part. But when that which is perfect is come, then that which is in part shall be done away.

2. **Mark 16:20** — And they went forth, and preached every where, the Lord working with them, and confirming the word with signs following. Amen.

3. **1 Corinthians 3:9** — For we are labourers together with God: ye are God's husbandry, ye are God's building.

SYNOPSIS

In this lesson, Rick and Tony address the question that has plagued many believers in the Body of Christ: *Does God still do miracles today?* By tackling this theological question with scripture, personal examples, historical proof, and research from Tony's book *Miracles and the Supernatural Throughout Church History*, they reveal how God's supernatural power has been and always will be a necessary part of a vibrant Christian life. The Holy Spirit is still at work today and will continue to move miraculously around the world through the Church until Jesus Christ returns.

The emphasis of this lesson:

Many in the Church have often wondered if miracles and the supernatural power of the Holy Spirit are still available today. Thankfully, the Word of God teaches that the gifts of the Spirit will be moving throughout the Church body until the time of the Lord's return. History also shows the Holy Spirit has been continually at work within the Church since the Day of Pentecost. Documented miracles have taken place over a 2,000 year period in regions all over the world including Ancient Asia, Northern Africa, Europe, and America. While some

believers approach the supernatural with a cessation viewpoint, true Bible-based theology presents a continual moving of God's presence and power. Miracles are vital to the demonstration of the Gospel message and are activated by faith in God and His Word.

Miracles and the Supernatural Are Still for Today

Many denominations teach that miracles and the gifts of the Spirit stopped with the death of the apostles. However, close examination of Scripture reveals an opposite theological position. In fact, the Bible teaches that God gave miracles and the gifts of the Spirit to be with the Church until Jesus returns. These supernatural demonstrations of God's power set people free and authenticate the preaching of the Gospel message.

A careful, thorough study of Church history also proves that God's power has been evident throughout the church age in every region touched by the Gospel. God's power is still working today, because His power has not changed or diminished. He's still doing the same thing today that He did yesterday — and what He does today, He'll be doing tomorrow. The Bible declares that Jesus is the same yesterday, today, and forever. The power of the Holy Spirit that was manifested on the Day of Pentecost is the same power flowing through the Church today!

Tony's Personal Testimony of Experiencing the Power of God

Like Rick, Tony also grew up in a denomination where the power of God was not taught or demonstrated. As a result of his upbringing, he had never personally encountered a supernatural touch of God. However, all that changed when he was 18 and attended a healing meeting where Reverend Charles and Frances Hunter were speaking.

Two years prior to that time, Tony had suffered a back injury from playing tennis. While the injury hadn't stopped him from playing sports, it had become a source of constant nagging pain. When Charles Hunter prayed for him that night, he felt the tangible power of God go into his body. He was instantly healed of all back pain!

Later, as Tony was studying Scripture, he remembered the Bible story recounting the healing of the woman with the issue of blood. The Bible states that the woman *felt* in her body that she was healed and Jesus had *felt* power going out of Him (*see* Mark 5:29,30). It was then that Tony understood how the power of the Holy Spirit can sometimes be tangibly felt when a healing or miracle is taking place.

After the Hunter meeting, Tony's friend introduced him to the baptism of the Holy Spirit. At first, he was a little hesitant because of the particular teaching he had received growing up in his denomination. He had heard about the Holy Spirit whenever he recited the Apostle's Creed or sang the Doxology, but he had never understood the full Person and work of the Holy Spirit. Thankfully, his friend led him through the book of Acts and showed him clearly from Scripture how believers were filled with the Holy Spirit and spoke in other tongues. On that night, Tony also received the baptism of the Holy Spirit. He has been walking in the blessing of knowing and experiencing God ever since!

The Bible says to "taste and see that the Lord is good" (*see* Psalm 34:8). Sadly, many people slip into a mode of Christianity that is solely theoretical, philosophical, or intellectual. While knowledge and information are good, they are not all that's included in Christianity. There is an experiential side to walking with the Lord that is required for a vibrant Christian life.

Tony's Academic Study That Led to His Book

While preparing for his Master's degree in Theological Studies with a Church History Cognate, Tony studied miracles and the supernatural as part of his coursework. He was introduced to several key characters in church history and became acquainted with resources documenting the supernatural move of God since the day of Pentecost. It was during this time of academic study that Tony was inspired to dig deeper into the evidence surrounding the experiential side of Christianity. His research eventually led him to write the book *Miracles and the Supernatural Throughout Church History*.

Historical research proves that in every century there have been groups of Christians who have experienced the power of God. Records indicate that healings, miracles, and gifts of the Spirit have been present throughout the church age. Moreover, the subtle workings of the Holy Spirit such as the conviction of sin and the new birth have not changed throughout the centuries. All throughout church history, the power and person of the Holy Spirit have remained the same.

The Gifts of the Spirit Are in the Church Until Jesus Returns

When it comes to the moving of the gifts of the Spirit, many believers have been taught erroneous doctrine due to misinterpretation of Scripture. One particular passage that often confuses believers is First Corinthians 13:8-10: "...But whether there be prophecies, they shall fail; whether there be tongues, they shall cease; whether there be knowledge, it shall vanish away. For we know in part, and we prophesy in part. But when that which is perfect is come, then that which is in part shall be done away."

Some denominations use this passage to suggest that the gifts of the Spirit ceased when the Bible was written or when the first apostles died. However, the phrase "that which is perfect" is not referring to the canonization of Scripture or to the passing of the foundational apostles. The full context of that passage is actually referring to the perfect time of when we see Jesus in heaven.

Once we see Jesus on the other side of eternity, we will fully know as we are fully known (*see* 1 Corinthians 13:12). Until that perfect time, we will continue to only know in part and prophecy in part. Therefore, based on the context of that Scripture, spiritual gifts will continue until the day of the Lord Jesus Christ. When we see Jesus, we will know everything. But until that moment happens, prophesies and tongues will continue operating in the Body of Christ.

Documented Proof of the Supernatural Throughout Church History

As Tony continued his research into church history, he came across many Early Church sources that documented a strand of miracles down through the centuries. Writers such as Irenaeus, Tertullian, and Justin Martyr documented all kinds of healings, deliverances from demonic power, and operations of diverse spiritual gifts. Some even recorded accounts of the dead being raised!

In later church history, preachers like John Wesley, D.L. Moody, and Spurgeon also documented the supernatural weaving through the Body of

Christ. In fact, Spurgeon was known to have moved in the word of knowledge, while Charles Finney and Jonathan Edwards described a move of the Holy Spirit across America. They even witnessed people falling under the power of God in their meetings.

History reveals a cord of miracles being woven into the very fabric of Christ's Body. Miracles and operations of the gifts of the Holy Spirit have never entirely disappeared from the Church. All through church history, the supernatural was present when people were hungry for God and expected Him to move in their midst.

Faith Activates Miracles

The Bible says that these signs shall follow those who believe (*see* Mark 16:17,18). When Christians engage their faith, they will see the power of God move. On the contrary, when the church becomes ritualistic and historical, some of the miraculous begins to dissipate. It is faith that ignites the power of God.

While God remains the same, people must cooperate with Him in their faith and expectancy in order for His power to be manifested. If Christians are simply doing life in their own energy and effort, they are not being open to the partnership and cooperation of the Holy Spirit. Paul said believers are to be laborers together with God. Mark 16:20 records the disciples going forth preaching everywhere as the Lord worked with them. The manifestation of God's power is a two-sided coin that requires God's unchanging power and the activation of a believer's faith in His Word.

Cessationist Vs. Continuationist

In approaching the topic of miracles, there are two opposing schools of thought: cessationist and continuationist. The word *cessation* comes from the word *cease*, which means *to stop*. When something ceases, it discontinues. Therefore, a cessationist is someone who believes that at some point in time — whether it was with the death of the last apostle or the formalizing of the canon of Scripture — the power of God stopped working in the Church. This school of thought believes that God withdrew the gifts of the Spirit, tongues, prophecy, healing, and miracles from the Church so that they are no longer working today.

On the contrary, a continuationist believes that the gifts of the Spirit and the power of God have not ceased but are continuing to operate in the Church. A continuationist believes that God's power has never changed because God has not changed His mind regarding the need for His power to be demonstrated in and through His Body.

A thorough investigation into church history reveals that God's power has not ceased from working in the Church but rather continues on to this day. Tony's book *Miracles and the Supernatural Throughout Church History* dives into the annals of Early Church records, historical documents, and personal research to uncover the thread of miracles weaving throughout the Body of Christ for the past 2,000 years. His study revealed that God's power has been present in every region including Asia, Asia Minor, North Africa, Europe, and America. From the first century to the twenty-first century, God's power has continued to change lives, heal sick bodies, deliver the oppressed, and fill believers with the Holy Ghost!

God Wants To Manifest His Power Today

God's power, might, and strength have not diminished over time, because the Bible says He is still the same yesterday, today, and forever. God still wants to manifest His power in the Church today. In fact, in this day and age when the world is getting darker and darker, Christians need His power more than ever before. The Church needs signs, wonders, miracles, and the power of the Holy Spirit. God has always desired to display His mighty power in and through His Body.

A.W. Tozer said if the Holy Spirit was withdrawn from the Church today, 95% of what we do would go on and no one would notice the difference. But if the Holy Spirit had been withdrawn from the New Testament church, 95% of what they did would stop and everybody would have known the difference. Christians need the power of God in the Church today!

It's important to remember that Jesus never changes and never will change. He is the Head of the Church, and His power is still available if believers will cooperate with Him by activating their faith in His Word. God is the Great I Am, not the Great I Was. By expecting Him to move among the Church today, Christians can experience a fresh outpouring of the Holy Spirit in a miraculous and mighty way.

STUDY QUESTIONS

Study to shew thyself approved unto God, a workman that needeth
not to be ashamed, rightly dividing the word of truth.
— 2 Timothy 2:15

1. First Corinthians 13:8-10 says, "...*But whether there be prophecies,
    they shall fail; whether there be tongues, they shall cease; whether there be
    knowledge, it shall vanish away. For we know in part, and we prophesy
    in part. But when that which is perfect is come, then that which is in part
    shall be done away.*" One day, that perfect time of seeing Jesus face to
    face will come, but until then, prophesies and tongues will continue
    operating in the Body of Christ. Until this lesson, were you under the
    impression that miracles and the supernatural had ceased working?
    How did this lesson strengthen your faith to believe God for more of
    His power in your life?

2. Mark 16:20 says, "*And they went forth, and preached everywhere, the
    Lord working with them, and confirming the word with signs follow-
    ing.*" How are you cooperating with the Lord in the preaching of
    the Gospel? Are you expecting God to confirm His Word with signs
    following?

3. First Corinthians 3:9 says, "*For we are laborers together with God: ye are
    God's husbandry, ye are God's building.*" In what ways are you laboring
    together with God in His plan for your life? Are you doing things on
    your own, or are you working with God in what He has called you to
    do?

PRACTICAL APPLICATION

But be ye doers of the word, and not hearers only,
deceiving your own selves.
— James 1:22

Expect God's unchanging power to be manifested in your life today.

1. Have you ever studied church history to discover how God demon-
    strated Himself in times past? What were your observations?

2. When did you first realize that God's power is still available for His
    Church today?

3. Think of a time when you personally experienced God's supernatural power in your life. How did this encounter with God's Spirit change you?

TOPIC

The Move of God in Ancient Asia

SCRIPTURES

1. **Acts 4:29,30 (NKJV)** — Now, Lord, look on their threats, and grant to Your servants that with all boldness they may speak Your word, by stretching out Your hand to heal, and that signs and wonders may be done through the name of Your holy Servant Jesus.

2. **Acts 8:5,6,8** — Then Philip went down to the city of Samaria, and preached Christ unto them. And the people with one accord gave heed unto those things which Philip spake, hearing and seeing the miracles which he did…And there was great joy in that city.

3. **1 Corinthians 1:7** — So that ye come behind in no gift; waiting for the coming of our Lord Jesus Christ.

SYNOPSIS

In this lesson, Rick and Tony continue their conversation about the power of the Holy Spirit throughout the church age. Using research from Tony's book *Miracles and the Supernatural Throughout Church History*, they uncover details of the Holy Spirit's magnificent working through the Early Church fathers in Ancient Asia. They note that while the Holy Spirit does move in spectacular ways, often times His power is demonstrated in subtle supernatural manifestations like repentance and deliverance from demonic powers. As long as faith is activated on the Word of God, the Holy Spirit will move mightily wherever hearts are open!

The emphasis of this lesson:

The power of the Holy Spirit has been working throughout the Church ever since the Day of Pentecost. In fact, documentation has proven that

supernatural workings and miracles have been flowing through believers all over the world since the Church age first began. This powerful demonstration of God's Spirit was first recorded in Jerusalem and then quickly matriculated to the next hotspot of the Gospel — Ancient Asia or modern-day Turkey. From Ephesus to Caesarea, God's power was made known to people all over that region for centuries. Respected Early Church fathers like Ignatius of Antioch, Gregory of Caesarea, and Gregory of Nyssa were known for spiritual manifestations that accompanied their preaching. As the Early Church expected the Holy Spirit to move in their midst, God demonstrated the preaching of His Word with many signs following.

The Region of Ancient Asia

When people hear the term Asia, they usually think about countries like China, India, or Japan. However, in early biblical times, Asia referred to the region known today as Turkey. Much of Paul's ministry centered in that area — he was born in Tarsus and he ministered in many of the provinces and cities of that region like Galatia and Ephesus. In fact, it was in the ancient Asian city of Antioch where believers were first called Christians and where missionaries were regularly sent out on Gospel missions.

The region of Ancient Asia — or what we could call Turkey today — was a hotbed for Gospel activity during the years of the Early Church. During the first, second, and third centuries, that area abounded with the work of God. In fact, many of the historical ruins mentioned in the Bible are located in Turkey.

One Asian city radically touched with the power of God during Paul's ministry was the ancient city of Ephesus. In fact, it has been noted that Paul's greatest ministry work was accomplished in this city. He lived in Ephesus longer than anyplace else, and it was here that he started a two-year Bible school that sent out multiple church planters throughout the region. The Bible also says that God worked special or unusual miracles through Paul during his ministry work in Ephesus (*see* Acts 19:11). The ministry in Ephesus was clearly supernatural!

Supernatural Isn't Always Spectacular

When the Holy Spirit moves among people, different types of miracles and manifestations may occur in various degrees of magnitude. Some miracles may be spectacular while others may be more subtle. No matter how outwardly astonishing a miracle may be, it's important to appreciate even the more ordinary workings of the Holy Spirit. The supernatural isn't always spectacular.

Believers often experience the usual manifestations of the Holy Spirit throughout their everyday life, even when they don't realize it. Examples of these subtle workings of the Holy Spirit may be when God miraculously sustains a person in a time of crisis, encourages him during a challenging time, connects him with others for Kingdom purpose, or illuminates his mind when he needs an answer. No matter how the Holy Spirit may work in a believer's life, every manifestation — whether subtle or spectacular — is something God does to bless His people. Believers are to be thankful for all the various ways in which the Holy Spirit demonstrates His power and sets people free.

Ignatius of Antioch

The moving of God's Spirit is recorded in the writings of Ignatius of Antioch, one of the early Christian historians. Originally one of John's disciples, Ignatius became the pastor of the church in the Ancient Asian city of Antioch around 80 AD. About 15 years later after John's death, Ignatius wrote a letter to Polycarp, a fellow disciple. In this letter, Ignatius told Polycarp to "ask that invisible things will be shown to you so that you will not lack anything and you will abound in every spiritual gift." Clearly, Ignatius and Polycarp both desired spiritual gifts in their ministry.

Later, Ignatius wrote letters to several believers while being transferred to Rome for execution. These letters are so powerful and full of the Spirit. In fact, one letter addressed to the believers at Rome detailed Ignatius' stand before his execution. He asked that the believers not do anything to interfere with his martyrdom. He wanted to die for Jesus. God gave him such supernatural grace and favor as he laid down his life for the Lord. That was truly a mighty working of the Holy Spirit!

The Power of God in Ephesus

Perhaps one of the most miraculous chapters of Paul's ministry took place in Ephesus, a major port city in Ancient Asia. So many supernatural manifestations happened there including deliverance from demonic power, healings, and great repentance. It was here that Paul prayed over handkerchiefs and sick people were healed when the cloths were laid on them (*see* Acts 19:12). The power of God was so strong in Ephesus that people who were involved in the occult were supernaturally delivered and set free. They even burned all their occult items and books!

Sometimes, Christians become so focused on the spectacular manifestations of the Spirit of God that they forget the other subtle yet tremendous ways in which God works. For example, repentance isn't always showy, but it is a mighty working of God's power. When people turn from wickedness, renounce their deeds of darkness, and turn to the Lord Jesus, that is supernatural! God is strongly at work when people come under the conviction of the Holy Ghost, repent of their sins, and are set free from the powers of darkness.

This is what happened in the city of Ephesus. Because the whole city was given over to idolatry, the people were held captive by the occult and demonic powers. There was a lot of dark, evil supernatural activity happening in Ephesus! However, when the power of God swept through that city, the supernatural convicting power of the Holy Ghost fell on people and brought them to a place of deliverance and repentance. They were translated from the kingdom of darkness into the kingdom of light. The light came, they received the knowledge of the Truth, the chains of darkness fell from them, and they were made alive in Christ Jesus. That is supernatural!

The preaching of the Word of God coupled with the power of the Holy Spirit is an extraordinary combination that sets even the most enslaved person free. When the authentic Gospel is preached and demonstrated, whole cities end up rejoicing in the newfound liberty of Christ. The move of God that marked Ephesus was so powerful that it literally launched ministers and new churches all over the region with the Gospel.

The Faith of the Early Church

One remarkable characteristic of the Early Church is that they had faith in the supernatural. Because ancient cultures were open to the realm of the spirit, early Christians did not find it difficult to expect God's supernatural power to manifest. On the contrary, today's Western culture promotes an analytical and philosophical belief structure. It was perhaps this difference in perception that helped to facilitate many miracles in the early days of the Church.

The expectation of God's power among the believers is clearly seen throughout the New Testament. The book of Acts especially records the miraculous events surrounding the lives and ministries of the first Christians. For example, Acts 4:29 records a powerful scenario where the disciples were just released from prison and came together with other believers for prayer. This is how they prayed: "Now, Lord, look on their threats, and grant to Your servants that with all boldness they may speak Your word, by stretching out Your hand to heal, and that signs and wonders may be done through the name of Your holy Servant Jesus." Despite the hardships facing them, these persecuted Christians continued to boldly preach the Gospel with supernatural signs following. They had tenacious faith!

Gregory of Caesarea

Another notable early Christian was a man named Gregory Thaumaturgus of Caesarea in Cappadocia, which is in modern-day Turkey. This man was born in 213 AD, years after the first apostles were gone from the scene. Gregory was well known for his supernatural ministry. In fact, his last name even meant "miracle worker." His contemporary, Basil of Caesarea — one of the most respected Early Church fathers — noted that Gregory's ministry was full of the Spirit and manifested the gift of prophecy and power over demons.

Gregory's ministry was so anointed that when he first went into the city of Caesarea, he found only 17 Christians. By the time he left the city, there were only 17 people there who were *not* Christians! The evangelistic thrust of his ministry was similar to that of Philip: "Then Philip when down to the city of Samaria, and preached Christ unto them. And the people with one accord gave heed unto those things which Philip spake, hearing and seeing the miracles which he did. …And there was great joy in that city" (Acts 8:5,6,8). Like Philip in Samaria, Gregory also experienced the same kind of supernatural results in his ministry in Caesarea.

Gregory of Nyssa

History includes the ministry of another significant Early Church father named Gregory of Nyssa. He was also known to have supernatural results in his ministry including healing and deliverance of demons. It is recorded that his ministry consisted of proclaiming, discerning, directing, teaching, and healing. Like so many other ministers of his day, Gregory of Nyssa was not a magician or sorcerer. He was first and foremost a preacher of the Gospel of the Lord Jesus Christ. When he preached the Gospel, the Lord confirmed the message with signs following.

What Gregory and the many Early Church fathers understood was the importance of working with and through the Holy Spirit in their ministry. They partnered together with the Holy Spirit as they preached the Word, and that is why so many of them had such strong spiritual manifestations (*see* Mark 16:20). None of them accomplished these things in their own strength; they were simply activating their faith with the Word they preached, and God did the rest.

Supernatural Manifestations are for Today

There are many, many records of people moving in the gifts of the Holy Spirit during the time of the Early Church in Ancient Asia. These manifestations occurred years after the first apostles died and continued to manifest in the lives and ministries of the believers in that region. Gregory of Nyssa, Gregory of Caesarea, and Ignatius of Antioch are just a few of the believers recorded in history that preached the Gospel of Jesus Christ with mighty signs following.

First Corinthians 1:7 says, "So that ye come behind in no gift: waiting for the coming of the Lord Jesus Christ." The supernatural manifestations will be with the Church until the coming of the Lord and the Church should be expecting them. This is the way God has set up His Church, and this is the way it will be until the end of the church age. The Holy Spirit does the same thing everywhere, and He will continue to do so as long as people are willing to cooperate with Him. Where hearts are opened, the Holy Spirit moves mightily!

> And when the stream of doctrine is gushing forth in the Church and a devout heart is welling up with the gifts of the Holy Spirit,

do you not gladly give your attention? Do you not receive this
favor with thanksgiving?

— Basil of Caesarea

STUDY QUESTIONS

> Study to shew thyself approved unto God, a workman that needeth
> not to be ashamed, rightly dividing the word of truth.
> — 2 Timothy 2:15

1. Acts 4:29 and 30 states, "Now, Lord, look on their threats, and grant
   to Your servants that with all boldness they may speak Your word, by
   stretching out Your hand to heal, and that signs and wonders may be
   done through the name of Your holy Servant Jesus." (*NKJV*) Take a
   moment to examine your heart. If you were being persecuted for your
   faith in Jesus, would you follow the disciple's example in the Bible and
   pray for more boldness to preach the Word with signs following? Or
   would you cave under the pressure?

2. Acts 8:5,6,8 says, "Then Philip went down to the city of Samaria, and
   preached Christ unto them. And the people with one accord gave
   heed unto those things which Philip spake, hearing and seeing the
   miracles which he did...And there was great joy in that city." After
   seeing examples of miracles in Scripture, how is your faith being
   strengthened to believe God for mighty demonstrations following the
   preaching of the Gospel?

3. First Corinthians 1:7 says, "So that ye come behind in no gift; waiting
   for the coming of our Lord Jesus Christ." The Bible teaches that the
   gifts of the Spirit will be in operation until the coming of Jesus. What
   gifts have you seen in operation in church or in your own personal life?

PRACTICAL APPLICATION

> But be ye doers of the word, and not hearers only,
> deceiving your own selves.
> — James 1:22

Cooperate with the Holy Spirit and watch God demonstrate the preaching of His Word.

1. The power of God was so strongly manifested in the Early Church that Ignatius of Antioch was supernaturally graced to lay down his life for Jesus. If you were in his position, would you be so full of God's Word that you would expect God's power to work in you and through you even in death?

2. One of the great testimonies that came from Paul's ministry in Ephesus were the numerous deliverances and salvations of people involved in the occult. How is your faith stirred to believe God to snatch people from the fires of occultism and to set them free by His supernatural power?

3. It is said that after Gregory of Caesarea preached Christ to the city, there were only 17 people left who were not born again. Take a moment to pray for your city and ask God to bring a wave of the Gospel where you live. Ask Him for an outpouring of His Spirit that demonstrates the preaching of the Gospel message. Expect Him to bring salvation to your city so that hardly anyone is left in darkness!

LESSON 3

TOPIC

The Move of God in Northern Africa

SCRIPTURES

1. **1 Corinthians 1:5-7** — That in every thing ye are enriched by him, in all utterance, and in all knowledge; Even as the testimony of Christ was confirmed in you: So that ye come behind in no gift; waiting for the coming of our Lord Jesus Christ.

2. **Romans 12:6** — Having then gifts differing according to the grace that is given to us...

3. **Mark 16:17** — And these signs shall follow them that believe...

SYNOPSIS

In this lesson, Rick and Tony continue their conversation about the power of the Holy Spirit throughout the church age. Using research from Tony's book *Miracles and the Supernatural Throughout Church History*, they uncover details of the Holy Spirit's magnificent working through the Early Church fathers in North Africa. They discuss three principle figures in the Early Church — Tertullian, Origen, and Augustine — and note the dynamic supernatural results each one of them experienced in their ministries. The Holy Spirit has never ceased from working in the Church, and He moves wherever and whenever He is embraced.

The emphasis of this lesson:

North Africa played a key role in Jesus' earthly life and in the days of the Early Church. Through the writings of Early Church fathers, believers can catch a glimpse of the wonderous working of the Holy Spirit in this ancient region. Notable men like Tertullian of Carthage, Origen of Alexandria, and Augustine of Hippo all experienced unusual manifestations of God's power as they preached the Gospel. Because they had simple faith in the power of the Holy Spirit, their preaching resulted in miraculous confirmations of the Gospel message of the Lord Jesus Christ.

Enriched by Him

While some parts of the Church teach that spiritual gifts and miracles have been done away with, the Bible teaches something entirely different. In fact, the Bible is so full of miracles and the workings of the Spirit that it's very difficult to preach a true Gospel message void of the supernatural. Moreover, a careful search of history proves that God's Spirit has been working in and through the Church all over the world since the Day of Pentecost. Anyone who teaches that miracles have disappeared from the Church have not experienced God's power — or, in some cases, he's being dishonest. Miracles have been and always will be a hallmark of the Gospel of Jesus Christ.

In teaching the Corinthian church about the supernatural workings of the Holy Spirit, Paul wrote, "That in every thing ye are enriched by him, in all utterance, and in all knowledge; Even as the testimony of Christ was confirmed in you: So that ye come behind in no gift; waiting for the coming of our Lord Jesus Christ" (1 Corinthians 1:5-7). Now, the Corinthian church was one of the most charismatic churches of Paul's day — they were known for their exuberance of the gifts of the Spirit. Yet, Paul instructed them that they should continue to be "enriched by Him in all utterance and knowledge."

The word "enriched" is a translation of the Greek word *plousios,* which is the origin for the English word "plutocrat." A plutocrat is someone so filthy stinking rich that he can't even figure out how much money he has. Because Paul used the word *plousios,* he was admonishing the Corinthian church to be so enriched by Him in all utterance and knowledge that they would literally be abounding with spiritual gifts. In other words, the Corinthian church was to be stinking rich when it came to spiritual manifestations!

Paul then went on to tell the church that they "come behind in no gift; waiting for the coming of our Lord Jesus Christ." Clearly, Paul was teaching the church that the gifts of the Holy Spirit are to be in operation until the end of the church age when Jesus comes back. Based upon this passage of Scripture, it's evident that God's supernatural power will be working in and through the Church until the return of the Lord.

North Africa in Scriptures

Many believers don't realize just how significant the region of North Africa is in the New Testament. In fact, North Africa serves as the backdrop for many key points in the life of Jesus and in the history of the Early Church. For instance, Egypt is where Joseph took Mary and baby Jesus to escape Herod's baby-killing rampage. As a result, Jesus spent the first three and a half to four years of his life in North Africa.

Later, when Jesus was crucified, there was a gentleman who stepped in to help carry His cross. This man was Simon of Cyrene. He was originally from modern-day Libya, which is located in North Africa.

Because the Roman Empire dominated so much of the world at that time, it brought people together from many diverse regions including North Africa. This convergence of nations is seen in Acts chapter 2 where people from Libya and Egypt were present in Jerusalem on the Day of Pentecost and heard the apostles praying in tongues. The story of the Antioch church in Acts 13 also depicts a wide gathering of many nations, including individuals from North Africa.

Finally, North Africa played a big role in the early move of God. Apostles like Mark, the author of the gospel of Mark, traveled to North Africa as missionaries. Records indicate he established a church in Alexandria, Egypt. And of course, there was the story of the Ethiopian eunuch who received the Gospel when Philip preached to him (*see* Acts 8). Considering all these biblical accounts, it's evident that North Africa played an important role in the early days of the New Testament Church.

Early Church Fathers

As the Gospel began to take root in North Africa, the church began to grow and flourish. Consequently, many notable ministers came out of that region and documented the history of the Early Church through their writings. These men are often called Early Church fathers.

The term "fathers" refers to certain church leaders that came after the apostolic era. In the first days of the church, men like Paul, Peter, and John were key leaders in the Body of Christ. After their deaths, another generation rose up to take the helm of leadership. These men wrote both prolifically and authoritatively. They were well educated, versed in multiple languages, and intellectually brilliant. More importantly, they were well acquainted with the Scriptures and with the Holy Spirit. These mighty leaders in the Early Church were very familiar with the power of God.

The Spirit-Filled Ministry of Tertullian

One of the most notable Early Church fathers from North Africa was a man by the name of Tertullian. He was born in the year 160 and died in the year 220. Much of his ministry took place in Carthage, which is modern-day Tunisia between Libya and Algeria. God's power was so present in his ministry that many men of high rank were delivered from devils and healed of diseases!

In Tertullian's writings, he acknowledged "spiritual charismata." This word *charismata* is the origin of the word *charismatic* or "gifts." In addition to his own recognition of the gifts of the Spirit, Tertullian went on to record many instances where those gifts were in manifestation. For example, one of the ladies in his church moved often in the gifts of the Spirit including word of knowledge, word of wisdom, discernment of spirits, and prophecy. Tertullian noted that "they recognize and honor the prophecies and recent visions" that were taking place among the believers of his day. God was still working in the Church and continuing to give people illumination, insight, and direction by the Holy Spirit.

Tertullian recognized the importance and place of the gifts of the Spirit. He discerned the authentic spiritual manifestations and didn't shy away from them. He even warned the Church that the gifts of the Spirit are tools, not toys. Long after the age of the apostles, Tertullian's writings provide evidence that the gifts of the Spirit were honored, respected, and operating in the Body of Christ. The early Christians, even in the third century, believed the gifts of the Spirit were part of the normal Christian life.

The Holy Spirit Moves Where He Is Expected

Romans 12:6 states, "Having then gifts differing according to the grace that is given to us...." Because the early Christians grabbed onto this passage in sincere faith and believed in the supernatural working of the Holy Spirit, they were not disappointed. History clearly depicts how powerful the Holy Spirit moved among them. The Holy Spirit will always move wherever He is expected!

Sadly, many people today have been taught that the gifts of the Holy Spirit have been done away with in the Church. Some believe that miracles are no longer for today or that the supernatural no longer exists. Because the traditions of man have been elevated in the minds and hearts of many in the Church, the Word of God doesn't have any effect on people that hold to such misconceptions. Far too many have been robbed of the gifts of the Spirit due to erroneous doctrine and unbelief. It takes faith in the Word of God to activate the miraculous. And when the Word of God is taught regarding the gifts of the Holy Spirit, miracles, and the supernatural workings of God, faith arises in people's hearts. Once faith is released, the supernatural ministry of the Holy Spirit begins to flow.

"And these signs shall follow them that believe..." (Mark 16:17). This is a promise from Jesus to His disciples regarding the supernatural power of God. Through faith, every Christian can activate this power in his or her life.

The Spirit-Filled Ministry of Origen

Another notable Early Church father from North Africa was a man named Origen, who also lived during the third century in Alexandria,

Egypt. Like Tertullian, he also recognized the importance of the Holy Spirit in the believer's life. His writings record this statement: "The name of Jesus can still remove distractions from the minds of men, expel demons, and also take away diseases; and produce a marvelous meekness of spirit and a complete change of character." Origen had a firm grasp on the fruit of the Spirit on one hand and the gifts of the Spirit on the other.

Almost every single Christian understands that the fruit of the Spirit hasn't ceased. Believers everywhere agree that the Holy Spirit within produces love, joy, peace, and a host of other Christ-like characteristics. If the same Holy Spirit is actively working today inside believers to bring forth the character of Jesus, how much more is He also actively working alongside believers to confirm the message of Jesus through supernatural gifts and miracles? Both the fruit and the gifts of the Holy Spirit are necessary for the work of Christ to continue on the earth today.

A firm believer in God's mighty power, Origen witnessed many wonderful testimonies of the Holy Spirit's work in the Early Church. He states, "I too have seen many persons freed from grievous calamities, from distractions of the mind, madness, and countless other ills that could not be cured by either men or devils." Origen understood the power in the name of Jesus! And that name still carries the same weight and power that it did in the early days of the Church.

Hindrances to the Supernatural

While the supernatural manifestations of the Holy Spirit have been documented throughout church history, some theologians still have a hard time accepting the truth. This disbelief may come from a lack of personal experience with the person and work of the Holy Spirit. Sometimes people don't believe certain things if they haven't personally experienced them. However, Scripture always settles the issue. If the Bible says it, then regardless of whether a person has experienced it or not, it still remains true.

Spiritual experiences should always coincide to some degree with the teachings of Scripture. God's Word declares that Jesus is the same yesterday, today, and forever. He never changes! Consequently, what a believer experiences should line up with the consistency of Scripture.

Reinhard Bonnke, a well-respected missionary to Africa in the twenty-first century, once said, "We have a supernatural Jesus, a supernatural

Bible, and a supernatural Gospel." As a result of this supernatural message, Christians should have no trouble believing in anything supernatural. When people use their Bible to say that miracles no longer exist, it's totally ridiculous because they're using a supernatural book! Sadly, they are refuting the very message the Bible communicates.

The Spirit-Filled Ministry of Augustine

Perhaps one of the most famous men in church history is another Early Church father from North Africa by the name of Augustine. In fact, many say that he is the most prolific scholar after the Apostle Paul. He is so popular in history and church culture that many things are often named after him including cities such as St. Augustine, Florida. Augustine came from a place called Hippo, which is modern-day Algeria. He died in the year 430 and so much of his ministry took place in the fifth century.

For many years, Augustine did not necessarily believe in miracles until he started seeing them. In his work *City of God*, he penned, "Even now, therefore, many miracles are worked, the same God who worked those we read of still performing them, by whom He will and as He will." Augustine documented 70 different miracles that occurred in the lives of his church members and stated that he couldn't even record all the miracles he knew. And all of those miracles took place in Africa!

God has always been a God of the miraculous, and what He did back then, even in the fifth century in Africa, He is still doing today. The Holy Spirit will always move when and where people expect Him. He will come with miraculous and supernatural power wherever He is embraced.

STUDY QUESTIONS

**Study to shew thyself approved unto God, a workman that needeth
not to be ashamed, rightly dividing the word of truth.
— 2 Timothy 2:15**

1. First Corinthians 1:5-7 says, "That in every thing ye are enriched by him, in all utterance, and in all knowledge; Even as the testimony of Christ was confirmed in you: So that ye come behind in no gift; waiting for the coming of our Lord Jesus Christ." Are you expecting to be enriched by Jesus in the gifts of the Spirit?

2. Romans 12:6 says, "Having then gifts differing according to the grace that is given to us...." What different gifts of the Spirit have you personally seen in operation?

3. Mark 16:17 says, "And these signs shall follow them that believe...." Recall a time when you saw a miracle or the gifts of the Spirit manifested. What scriptures were being preached that built faith in people for the miraculous?

PRACTICAL APPLICATION

> But be ye doers of the word, and not hearers only,
> deceiving your own selves.
> —James 1:22

Preach the Gospel and expect the Holy Spirit to confirm the message.

1. Have you ever studied Early Church history? Were you aware of the Holy Spirit's power moving among the churches after the apostolic age?

2. When you share the Gospel with someone, do you expect the Holy Spirit to confirm the message of Jesus in power?

3. Early Church fathers like Tertullian, Origen, and Augustine had simple faith in the power of the Holy Spirit. What did you learn from their example?

LESSON 4

TOPIC

The Move of God in Europe

SCRIPTURES

1. **Mark 16:17** — And these signs shall follow them that believe...

2. **Hebrews 2:4** — God also bearing them witness, both with signs and wonders, and with divers miracles, and gifts of the Holy Ghost, according to his own will.

3. **Acts 1:8** — But ye shall receive power, after that the Holy Ghost is come upon you: and ye shall be witnesses unto me both in Jerusalem,

and in all Judea, and in Samaria, and unto the uttermost parts of the
earth.

4. **John 14:12** — …He that believeth on me, the works that I do shall he
    do also; and greater works than these shall he do; because I go unto
    my Father.

SYNOPSIS

In this lesson, Rick and Tony continue their conversation about the power
of the Holy Spirit throughout the church age. Using research from Tony's
book *Miracles and the Supernatural Throughout Church History*, they uncover
details of the Holy Spirit's magnificent working through the Early Church
fathers in Europe. They discuss principle figures in church history including the Apostle Paul, Irenaeus, Martin Luther, and John Wesley and note
the supernatural influence each one had on the European continent. The
same Holy Spirit that worked in the historical days of the Church is still
working in the Church today!

The emphasis of this lesson:

**Europe was first introduced to the Gospel by the Apostle Paul during
his travels to ancient Macedonia. Years after Paul's death, other great
ministers arose in that region including Irenaeus of Lyons. While many
consider Europe a spiritually dark continent, it has a rich heritage in the
Gospel. Men like Martin Luther and John Wesley were great leaders in
the Church and taught the Word of God in power with signs following.**

Diverse Miracles

All throughout church history, God's power has been on active display
through tremendous miracles, the gifts of the Spirit, and supernatural
manifestations. Every continent that has been touched by the Gospel has
at one time experienced a move of God's Spirit. History has proven that
whenever people engage their faith with the teachings of Scripture, God
responds in a mighty, supernatural way.

Hebrews 2:4 declares, "God also bearing them witness, both with signs
and wonders, and with divers miracles, and gifts of the Holy Ghost,
according to his own will." According to this verse, God moves supernaturally to bear witness to the Gospel message with signs, wonders, gifts of
the Spirit, and diverse miracles. Interestingly, the word "divers" used in this

passage is the same word used in the Old Testament Greek Septuagint to describe Joseph's coat of many colors. His coat was "variegated" or made up of diverse color patterns. In the same way, miracles can come in a variety of categories. They are variegated or diverse.

Miracles are amazing and show up in all kinds of sundry colors. The great diversity of them reveal God's heart to meet the many different needs of people and to demonstrate the depth of His love to mankind. Miracles have never ceased from the life of the Church, and they are still available for people today!

Paul's Ministry in Philippi

Jesus told His disciples to go into all the world, preach the Gospel to every creature, and to make disciples of all nations. In Acts 1:8, Jesus said, "But ye shall receive power, after that the Holy Ghost is come upon you: and ye shall be witnesses unto me both in Jerusalem, and in all Judea, and in Samaria, and unto the uttermost parts of the earth." Not only is God wanting to do miracles in time, all through history, but in every land and to every nation.

The move of God on the continent of Europe began with Paul's first trip to Philippi, the leading city in ancient Macedonia. This is the first biblical account of the Gospel reaching Europe. Originally, Paul was planning on going into Ephesus and other parts of Asia, but the Lord gave him a vision and supernaturally directed him to Macedonia (*see* Acts 16:10).

Once Paul arrived in Philippi, the Lord confirmed His Word with many supernatural signs. A slave girl was delivered from demon possession, Paul and Silas were supernaturally set free from prison, and the jailer and his whole household came to know the Lord. As the apostles entered the European continent boldly preaching the Gospel, the Holy Spirit moved mightily in their midst!

Irenaeus of Lyons

After the Gospel was established in Europe, other notable ministers continued to preach the Lord Jesus with power in that region. One such minister was a man named Irenaeus who was sent to the region by Polycarp, one of John's disciples. Polycarp had heard that there was a need for spiritual leadership in a church in Gaul, the region of modern-day France. To help bring spiritual stability to the church, he sent Irenaeus to the ancient city of Lyons. To this day, Irenaeus is often referred to as "Irenaeus of Lyons" because of his ministry in the city of Lyons, France.

Interestingly, Irenaeus recorded many supernatural events in his writings, including deliverance from demons. In fact, that is a prominent theme in some of his works. He noted, "For some truly drive out devils, so that those who have been cleansed from evil spirits, frequently both believe in Christ and join themselves to the church."

The power to cast out demons was a significant element of Jesus' earthly ministry, and it was prevalent in the days of the Early Church. Obviously, this supernatural manifestation is still available for the Church today. Sadly, many people in today's culture tend to self-medicate as a means not to feel vexed or oppressed — instead of believing God for deliverance. But demonic activity is just as real today as it was during the time of Jesus, the apostles, and the Early Church fathers. The power to cast out demons is still part of the supernatural ministry of the Gospel!

In his writings, Irenaeus also discussed several other supernatural manifestations that took place in his ministry including healing of the sick, raising the dead, demonstrations of the gifts of the Spirit, utterances of prophecy, and speaking in tongues. All of these instances are documented in his writings and detail the spiritual vibrancy of the Early Church in Europe.

Other Notable Early Church Fathers in Europe

While many consider Europe a spiritually dark continent, the church in that region was actually birthed in great power. Even after the days of the apostles, other powerful church leaders arose and ministered all over the region. In addition to Irenaeus of Lyons, there was Hilary of Poitiers, Martin of Tours, Gregory the Great, Augustine of Canterbury, and Bernard of Clairvaux. All of these men were known to preach the Gospel in power and demonstration.

Another Early Church father from France was Peter Waldo, who founded a group called the Waldensians. Records indicate that he believed in praying for the sick and anointing with oil. Like so many in the Early Church, Peter Waldo was just a doer of the Word of God — he believed God's Word and acted upon it. As a result of his faith, God showed up.

Martin Luther and the Reformation

One of the most well-known figures of European church history is Martin Luther, a key leader of the Protestant Reformation. He was born in 1483 in Germany and is celebrated for his message on justification by faith. He had a revelation from the Bible that people are not saved by works but by grace.

In addition to his Bible-based preaching, Martin Luther also experienced supernatural manifestations in his ministry including deliverance of demons and healing of the sick. He wrote, "Often it has happened and still does that devils have been driven out in the name of Christ. Also, by calling on His name and prayer, the sick have been healed."

Martin Luther was so familiar with the power of God that even one of his top associate ministers, Philip Melanchthon, said that he was healed from a terminal sickness because of Martin Luther's prayers. Another friend of Luther's, Friedrich Myconius, was also delivered from the point of death as a result of his prayers. In a letter to Myconius, Luther wrote, "I command you in the Name of God to live, because I still have need of you in the work of reforming the church. The Lord will never let me hear that you are dead, but will permit you to survive me. For this I am praying this is my will, and may my will be done, because I seek only to glorify the name of God." When Myconius received the letter, he was miraculously healed. In fact, he outlived Luther by two years!

A careful study of Martin Luther's life indicates he was a man thoroughly convinced of the reality of God's supernatural power. In fact, one of Luther's messages centered on the words of Jesus found in John 14:12: "He that believeth on me, the works that I do shall he do also; and greater works than these shall he do; because I go unto my Father." In a commentary on this passage, Luther wrote, "Therefore, we must allow these words to remain and not gloss over them as some have done who have said that these signs were manifestations of the Spirit in the beginning of the Christian era and that they have ceased. That is not right for the same power is in the church still."

John Wesley in England

Another major leader in European church history is John Wesley, founder of the Methodist Church. He was an Anglican from the Church of England. He was also an ordained priest, an Oxford graduate, and an Oxford professor. He had such an influence on the Church that 35 different denominations find their roots in his teachings!

John Wesley's encounter with the Holy Spirit began when he visited a charismatic group of Christians in Germany called the Moravians. He spent two months with the Moravians, attending meetings and being saturated in that powerful spiritual atmosphere. When he came back from his time there, he wrote about the meetings saying, "At about three in the morning, as we were continuing instant in prayer, the power of God came mightily upon us in so much that many cried out for exceeding joy and many fell to the ground." The Holy Spirit was so present among this group of people that many were falling out under the power of God.

Records indicate that many were healed under Wesley's ministry as well. In fact, Wesley once received a letter from a gentleman accusing him of claiming that people were getting healed in his meetings. Wesley replied, "As it can be proved by abundance of witnesses that these cures were frequently, indeed almost always the instantaneous consequences of prayer, your inference is just. I cannot, dare not, affirm that they were purely natural. I believe they were not. I believe many of them were wrought or produced by the supernatural power of God." Evidently, John Wesley's ministry was full of healing manifestations!

Engaged Faith

Studies in church history have revealed that God's power was always prevalent whenever people believed and acted upon the Word of God. God has always wanted to move by His power in the Church, and He is still wanting to move in churches today. He has not changed, for the Bible says Jesus is the same yesterday, today, and forever. What God did in the days of old, He still can and will do in modern day.

The secret to the miraculous is *engaged faith*. God will move for anyone that will engage their faith. Miracles are available for anyone who will simply believe. God will unleash His power wherever and whenever He is welcomed and received. The Charismatic Move isn't a new thing; it's something God has been doing since the Day of Pentecost!

STUDY QUESTIONS

Study to shew thyself approved unto God, a workman that needeth
not to be ashamed, rightly dividing the word of truth.
— 2 Timothy 2:15

1. Mark 16:17 says, "These signs shall follow them that believe." What are some biblically based signs that follow those that believe the Word of God?

2. Hebrews 2:4 says, "God also bearing them witness, both with signs and wonders, and with divers miracles, and gifts of the Holy Ghost, according to his own will." Interestingly, the word "divers" used in this passage is the same word used in the Old Testament Greek Septuagint to describe Joseph's coat of many colors. His coat was "variegated" or made up of diverse color patterns. What kinds of diverse or variegated miracles have you personally seen or heard about?

3. John 14:12 says, "He that believeth on me, the works that I do shall he do also; and greater works than these shall he do; because I go unto my Father." Are you actively engaging your faith with this passage of Scripture?

PRACTICAL APPLICATION

But be ye doers of the word, and not hearers only,
deceiving your own selves.
—James 1:22

Activate God's power in your life by believing His Word.

1. Before this lesson, were you aware of Europe's spiritual heritage? Why was the power of God so prevalent in the ministry of Paul, Irenaeus, Martin Luther, and John Wesley?

2. John Wesley had received many healing testimonies throughout his ministry. What healing do you need in your body, and are you actively believing God for healing based on His Word?

3. Many Early Church fathers reported several instances of demonic deliverances in their ministry. Why do you think people in modern culture do not receive deliverance from demonic power as much as they did in days past?

TOPIC

The Move of God in America

SCRIPTURES

1. **1 Corinthians 1:5-7**— That in every thing ye are enriched by him, in all utterance, and in all knowledge; Even as the testimony of Christ was confirmed in you; So that ye come behind in no gift; waiting for the coming of our Lord Jesus Christ.

SYNOPSIS

In this lesson, Rick and Tony continue their conversation about the power of the Holy Spirit throughout the church age. Using research from Tony's book *Miracles and the Supernatural Throughout Church History*, they uncover details of the Holy Spirit's magnificent working through well-known church leaders in early American history. They discuss principle figures such as John Wesley, Charles Spurgeon, Jonathan Edwards, and Charles Finney and note how they each embraced the demonstration of the Holy Spirit. America has been blessed with the First Great Awakening and the Second Great Awakening in the early years of her existence; she is now ready for a powerful new season of God's mighty outpouring!

The emphasis of this lesson:

America has been seeded with the truth of the Gospel since her inception. Many preachers like John Wesley, Charles Spurgeon, Jonathan Edwards, and Charles Finney have influenced America with their bold, anointed preaching. As a result of their hunger for God's Word and His Spirit, they saw many salvations, wonderful miracles, and demonstrations of God's power. The Old Testament prophet Joel foretold of a time when God would pour out His Spirit on all flesh. America has enjoyed the fruits of the First and Second Great Awakening in years past, but God is wanting to pour out of His Spirit afresh and anew in today's generation.

Abounding in the Gifts of the Spirit

According to the Bible, the gifts of the Spirit are to be active in the Church until the time of the Lord's return. An example of this is found in the Early Church at Corinth. In his letter to the charismatically active Corinthian church, Paul writes, "That in every thing ye are enriched by him; in all utterance, and in all knowledge; Even as the testimony of Christ was confirmed in you; So that ye come behind in no gift; waiting for the coming of our Lord Jesus Christ" (1 Corinthians 1:5-7).

The word "enriched" used in this passage is the Greek word *plousios*, which means to be filthy, stinking rich. By using the word *plousios*, Paul was emphasizing that the Corinthian church was rich with the gifts of the Holy Spirit. They were abounding with them! This church was so enriched in all kinds of spiritual gifts that they were overflowing. Utterance gifts and knowledge gifts were abundant in their congregation!

John Wesley

One notable minister that had great influence on the church in the United States was a man named John Wesley. While Wesley's ministry focused mainly in Europe, his influence reached America through the Methodist group that he founded. In addition to his anointed preaching, his ministry also included various demonstrations of the Holy Spirit. Records indicate that healings were not uncommon in his time. In fact, one man in particular, Mr. Myrick, appeared to have been raised from the dead!

In addressing the legacy of the Holy Spirit's power in his followers, Wesley made this statement: "I am not afraid that the people called Methodists should ever cease to exist either in Europe or America. But I am afraid lest they should only exist as a dead sect. Having the form of religion without the power. And this undoubtedly will be the case unless they hold fast both the doctrine, Spirit, and discipline with which they first set out."

Wesley understood that in order for the Church to move forward, the power of God must not diminish. He also recognized that if believers didn't maintain their commitment to the things of God, Jesus would remove the "candlestick", the fire of the Holy Spirit, from them. Wesley knew that denominations or groups of people can be birthed in the power of the Holy Spirit but can lose their fire over time if they don't contend for the fullness of God's Spirit.

In his writings, Wesley also addressed why some churches do not experience the power of God like they should. He said that because many Christians often grow cold in their love for God, the power and presence of the Holy Spirit become less prevalent among their midst. Some Christians lose so much of their commitment to Christ that they have no more of the Spirit than the heathens do. According to Wesley, this was a key reason as to why many believers who once knew the power of God begin to experience it less and less. The miracles never cease, but sadly, miraculous faith among believers often decreases. The Apostle Paul spoke about the work of faith — it takes *work* to stay in faith and to keep faith alive.

Charles Spurgeon

Another great minister that influenced American Christianity is Charles Spurgeon, often considered the prince of preachers. He was a famous Baptist minister and prolific writer. What many people don't know about him is that he operated in the gift of the word of knowledge. God would often supernaturally show him something about someone even when he was in the middle of preaching!

In fact, one time while Spurgeon was preaching, he pointed to a part of the sanctuary and said that a man had just come in with a bottle of gin in his pocket. Because of the supernatural manifestation of the gifts of the Spirit, that particular man repented and got saved. On another occasion, Spurgeon was preaching and pointed to a section in the church and said there was someone who had stolen a pair of gloves from his employer. Sure enough, after the service, a man confessed everything to Spurgeon and repented of his sin.

Jonathan Edwards

Perhaps one of the most well-known ministers in the early days of American history was Jonathan Edwards. A leading figure in the first Great Awakening, Edwards was well accustomed to revival meetings. Edwards was a brilliant theologian and scholar and became President of Princeton University shortly before he died. He is famous for his sermon *Sinners in the Hands of an Angry God* and preached often about God's mercy and the conviction of sin.

Around 1733, revival began breaking out in his church in Massachusetts. In fact, a wave of God's Spirit swept through the entire New England area, and the people of that region experienced a great revival. Edwards commented that the whole town of North Hampton seemed to be full of the presence of God. There was scarcely a single person in town, old or young, left unconcerned about the great things of the eternal world.

During these times of revival preaching, many people would fall under the power of God or be out in some kind of trance — sometimes as long as 24 hours! When they would come to, they would recount their experience with God. Lives were dramatically changed and transformed as a result of this mighty outpouring.

In addressing the issue of people falling out under the power, Edwards stated, "It is not at all strange that God should sometimes give his saints such foretaste of heaven as to diminish their bodily strength." These unusual manifestations paralleled certain instances in Scripture where people often fell down when coming into contact with the power of God. For example, when Saul of Tarsus encountered Jesus on the road to Damascus, he fell to the ground. In Revelation 1, John fell to his feet when he encountered Jesus the Risen Christ. While these outward manifestations seem strange to the natural human thinking, they are completely substantiated by both Scripture and historical evidence.

Because Edwards wanted people to know the difference between the counterfeit displays of the flesh and the genuine demonstrations of the Holy Spirit, he continued to address the supernatural manifestations in his book called *Distinguishing Marks of a Work of the Spirit of God*. In this work, he detailed how to recognize the authentic moves of the Holy Spirit. He said that first of all, a genuine demonstration must exalt Jesus as Lord and Savior. Second, it will work against the kingdom of Satan and his influence such as lust and sin. Third, it will stimulate a greater regard for the Holy Scripture. In other words, if something is truly marked by the Spirit, it will lead people to the Bible and not away from it. Fourth, it will promote the "Spirit of Truth." And finally, a true work of God will produce love for God and love for people.

Charles Finney

Another well-known minister of American history was Charles Finney, a dignified attorney from New England who was a key leader in the Second Great Awakening. When commenting on his experience with the baptism of the Holy Spirit, Finney wrote, "I received a mighty baptism of the Holy Ghost. The Holy Spirit descended upon me in a manner that seemed to go through me, body and soul. I could feel the impression, like a wave of electricity, going through me. It seemed to come in waves of liquid love, for I could not express it in any other way."

Finney also had several testimonies of the supernatural taking place in his ministry. One of his early experiences happened when he heard about a woman who was on the brink of death. He was so overcome by this news that when he began to pray, all he could do was groan in prayer. The next morning, he received news this woman was healed! It was also reported that hundreds of people would fall to the ground under the power of the Spirit during Finney's meetings.

Modern Day Notable Outpourings of the Holy Spirit

The last 100 years have seen several major outpourings of the Holy Spirit including the Azusa Street Revival in the early 1900s, the Healing Revival of the 1940s and 1950s, and the Charismatic Move of the 1960s and 1970s. Interestingly, about the same time the Azusa Street Revival began, another revival broke out on the other side of the world in Pyongyang, Korea. These various outpourings of the Holy Spirit have produced more than 600 million charismatics worldwide! That's over 600 million people who claim they have had an experience with the Holy Spirit and speak with other tongues.

The Old Testament prophet Joel prophesied that in the last days God would pour out His Spirit on all flesh. There is no doubt that time is upon the earth now. This great outpouring of the Holy Spirit will only continue to increase as the time of the Lord draws near.

God wants to pour out His Spirit on all flesh. He desires to meet people in their homes, in their families, and on their jobs. He wants to invade churches all over the world. Thankfully, there will be another Great

Awakening at the end of the age, and many will experience the glorious outpouring of the Holy Spirit!

STUDY QUESTIONS

> Study to shew thyself approved unto God, a workman that needeth
> not to be ashamed, rightly dividing the word of truth.
> — 2 Timothy 2:15

1. First Corinthians 1:5-7 says, "That in every thing ye are enriched by him; in all utterance, and in all knowledge; Even as the testimony of Christ was confirmed in you; So that ye come behind in no gift; waiting for the coming of our Lord Jesus Christ." Are you seeing the promise of this Scripture fulfilled in your life?

2. Acts 9 tells the story of Paul's conversion on the road to Damascus. Did you notice how Paul (also known as Saul of Tarsus) physically responded when he encountered Jesus? Have you ever experienced the power of God in such a tangible way that you couldn't stand up on your feet?

3. Joel 2:28,29 says, "And it shall come to pass afterward, that I will pour out my spirit upon all flesh; and your sons and your daughters shall prophesy, your old men shall dream dreams, your young men shall see visions: And also upon the servants and upon the handmaids in those days will I pour out my spirit." Have you experienced the power of the Holy Spirit in your own life?

PRACTICAL APPLICATION

> But be ye doers of the word, and not hearers only,
> deceiving your own selves.
> — James 1:22

Activate your faith for a fresh outpouring of the Holy Spirit in the world today.

1. Miracles never cease, but sadly, miraculous faith among believers often decreases. Has your faith been weak in the area of miracles? How can you strengthen your faith today to believe God for big miracles?

2. Charles Finney beautifully described his experience of being baptized in the Holy Spirit. How would you describe your own experience with the Holy Spirit?

3. Jonathan Edwards wrote about five things that distinguish a genuine work of the Holy Spirit. Using these wise guidelines, can you think of some supernatural experiences you've witnessed that were genuine demonstrations of the Holy Spirit?

NOTES

Cooke, Tony. *Miracles and the Supernatural Throughout Church History: Remarkable Manifestations of the Holy Spirit from the First Century Until Today.* Shippensburg, PA: Harrison House Publishers, 2020.

www.ingramcontent.com/pod-product-compliance
Lightning Source LLC
Chambersburg PA
CBHW071759020426
42331CB00008B/2328